From The Inside Out . . .

Recovering
from Workaholism

by
Barbara Hawkins

Printed by
TRI-STATE PRESS
Clayton, Georgia 30525

Dedication

To you who dare read about this topic.

To you, who gift others with this book; remember
"If you spot it, you got it!"

Acknowledgments

Appreciation is extended to all who have
encouraged this writing and all who have
been a part of its production; Anne, the
Thursday morning Living Process Group, the
women in the twelve step workshop, Bill,
Clay, Erin, and especially my parents. They
did their best with what they knew. Without
their influence and that of school, church
and society, I would not have found myself
on a recovery journey. I am grateful.

ISBN: 0-932298-74-5

Manufactured in the United States of America by
TRI-STATE PRESS
Clayton, Georgia 30525

Contents

THE PROCESS OF COMING TO THIS WRITING

As I walked in the hot steamy Indiana woods in July, I mused how much of my life had evolved and been involved with workaholism. I thought what a sacred cow work addiction is in this country. I know my experiences and I do not know all experiences with work addiction. I know how hard the recovery process is in a society which worships long work weeks and productivity.

Three months later in my office in a Thursday morning Living Process Group, I was sharing about my recovery process around work addiction and joked (I thought) about writing a book about workaholism. One of the participants, took my comment seriously. I was caught with her response. I was aware of a huge growing fear in the pit of my stomach. The fear quickly spread to a familiar knotted place in my throat. My heart beat fast as tears began to flow. I was encouraged by a co-facilitator to get in touch with how it felt to try to control my fear. "Terrible", I responded, and with that I was completely in touch with my feelings and not aware of the room and the people there. I felt myself travel through the terror and fear to a time long past in Scotland. There I had written poetic prose and often read my work to small assemblies. I was a left-handed

5

prolific scribe and quite popular in my time. As I moved into this knowing, the terror disappeared and a warm place glowed in my center. I knew I was to write from this space and not from my head. I knew I was to write about workaholism which I had experienced from all sides and edges of the coin.

I trusted the information. It didn't matter to me whether the experience would be validated by others. The information I received was important and directive. Throughout the following month during my writing time, I responded from my center. When it glowed warm, I wrote. I wrote about what other's work addiction experience triggered in my own memory, and I noted my frequent flashes about my own work addiction.

I spoke with many friends about my ideas and received much support and encouragement for which I am grateful. I spoke with Anne Wilson Schaef about writing and she was also very supportive. As I come to the close of this writing, I can feel the book move away from me. I am aware there is a letting go of this writing as it is not something I own. I am aware of myself moving on.

Allen Watts, a 1930 author, summarizes what I have learned. "The human being is not a thing but a process, not an object but life."

WORKAHOLISM IS . . .
THE PROCESS OF THE DISEASE

In *Co-Dependence Misunderstood-Mistreated,* Anne Wilson Schaef, describes the addictive process as underlying all addictive behavior and other sub-diseases in the areas of chemical dependency, mental health, women's movement, and family therapy. From her writing, I understand the addictive process to be active for me when I use focus on people, places, tasks or things as a way of leaving myself or escaping from painful parts of my past or present.

Workaholism is compulsive work, busyness, and doing; and is an expression of the addictive process in my life. I use workaholism to deal with the pain of abandoning myself and to increase my illusion of control. My workaholism began when I left who I experienced myself to be and that leaving occured very early in my life. In a later chapter the relationship between the addictive process and my own story will illustrate the early invasion of the disease process.

Workaholism comes historically out of the process of the people in our country moving from a survivalism mentality through pioneer times into a space of convenience and availability of leisure time. With the increase of leisure time, some people choose to fill their time with a survival mentality instead of feeling and being.

Survival mentality is fear based. It is "keeping the wolf away from the door." Survival mentality is working "as if." Pioneers worked as if the enemy were behind every tree, as if there wouldn't be enough, as if you survived or died. This may have been true.

However, modern people working as if the enemy were around every corner, as if there will not be enough, as if you survive or die, can become workaholics. They are too busy to notice or question. The fear may not be their own. This process of letting go of feelings, assumptions and beliefs that are not ours and belong in the past is evolution of the human consciousness. We get in trouble when we attempt to live and solve problems using old tools or respond to our world in rigid ways. The resulting pain can lead to addiction and disease.

Workaholism supports the addictive society and the addictive society supports workaholism. Every hero in America is a workaholic. Think about your heroes.

Characteristics of the Disease of "Doitis" and Workaholism

5:15 a.m. — It is 5:15 a.m. and at the sound of the alarm, my mind flashes with the day's agenda just like a computer.

5:30 a.m. — I'm up early so I can have some time alone. I feel low spiritually so I try to read my Bible and promise myself more church involvement.

6:00 a.m. — I rush to the Early Bird Fitness class at the YMCA. Stress management is my time, time for me! I watch others perform in the class and compare my performace. I must do more. I must do better.

7:00 a.m. — I literally rush home to make a good breakfast for my family. I really am doing it all! "I am feeling sick today," says my 12 year old. I hurriedly place a hand on his forehead. I tell myself he doesn't have a high fever and send him on to school with instructions to go to the nurse's office if he gets worse. I try not to look when I see him vomit on the grass before boarding the school bus. I *must* be at work today.

7:30 a.m. — With both children on the bus I speed to the office and

7:35 a.m. — unlock the building. Why am I always the first to arrive and the last to leave? I make two trips carrying in my "homework" from the previous night and my gym clothes and multiple lists and notes. I quickly check my 60 hour work-week schedule and ask, "Where is the coffee? Why do I feel so tired?"

8:00 a.m. — I move through back-to-back counseling sessions with four clients, leaving no time to note in their charts, return phone calls or go to the restroom.

12:00 p.m. — I race to the bathroom, my bladder in pain from drinking coffee all morning. "Why do I wait so long", I sigh. Speed counts at noon. I run to the post office, bank and dry cleaners. I pick up a few groceries for tonight and eat my lunch in the car while I interview a woman for a typing position. She tells me this is the first time she has ever been interviewed in a car. I tell myself how efficient I am. I can't remember what she looks like.

1:00 p.m. — I move through two client's sessions and feel warm and close to them as they focus on their problems. I feel powerful as I offer solutions to their problems.

3:00 p.m. — Oh no! A no-show! Now I have a whole hour to kill. I go to the restroom and return to my desk and begin moving paper piles into different places on my desk, pull some folders marked "future projects" and brainstorm elaborate workshops I never present.

4:00 p.m. — My client shows and I disappear for an hour into her problem area.

5-6:30 p.m. — I try to accomplish notations in the files of my clients and do not succeed. I clean my desk out and reorganize book shelves. I feel like a car spinning it's wheels, and know I need to go home and I can't seem to move in that direction.

6:30 p.m. — Somehow I spring out the door loading paperwork and books for tonight into my car. I toss a salad as soon as I'm home and serve a Crockpot meal to my family. I feel irritated at my family for not noticing my tiredness

7:00 p.m. — and not offering help. I clean up the kitchen, listing groceries which need replacing, run two loads of laundry and race out the door to the store.

8:30 p.m. — Home again, breathless. I dry laundry and fold clothes. Visually I check on the children. I tell myself, "They are so independent" and I do not really notice them.

9:30 p.m. — I shower and attempt to read and do paper work from the office, nodding off as I try to focus my eyes to read.

10:00 p.m. — My husband kisses me goodnight. I stay up another hour until I am finished with my work and then fall into a fitful sleep as my mind review's the day's work too loudly for real rest to occur.

Characteristics of compulsive doing and workaholism are elusive and evolve as the disease progresses through various stages. This list is partial. You may add your own comments as they occur to you. Workaholics will be tempted to read the table of contents, skip to the section on characteristics, and move quickly on to the recovery section. Workaholics will be reading with pen or underliner poised in hand because many of us use reading to numb out. We know we are mostly letting the words run through our heads like static on a radio. When we underline or write something in the margin we feel in control or efficient. My invitation to you as the reader is to spend some time reflecting on what you know about your own doing and working and to enter that in the spaces that are provided.

1. Lack of denial. Workaholics readily admit and name their work addiction. Unlike other addictions where one denies or delays identifying their addiction, workaholics often brag about the number of hours they work or label themselves proudly as workaholics.

2. Delusion. Workaholics often delude themselves that they are not hurting themselves or those with whom they are in primary relationships. The pain of isolation for the family of a workaholic is like living with an abusive person, loving and being dependent on her and afraid to leave her in spite of the pain in staying. Workaholics deny fear as their focus on tasks pulls them into the present instead of the fearful future. Workaholics deny feeling alone or abandoned.

3. Compulsion. Compulsion to work, to do, to move is always present. Making lists of tasks begin in the mind and often in bed when one is waking in the morning. Being stuck in work and not knowing when to quit becomes part of the compulsion. The antithesis of "you never finish what you start", workaholics unrealistically set goals for themselves and others. They agree to deadlines that are not possible to achieve. They have difficulty saying no. Many never say no. Workaholics have shades of perfectionism which is often heard as, "If you want something done right, do it yourself." Workaholics have a compulsive need to order their world, others and objects. This compulsive need to order helps with

the illusion of control. Something wrong? Let's do something! The doing takes away the scare and promotes feelings of control, power, importance and being one-up.

4. Non-feeling is part of the workaholic disease. We can use feelings to let ourselves know when we have had enough or when other people are using or abusing us. This option is not available to workaholics when they numb their feelings with doing and work. Sometimes workaholics may notice they are feeling very much as if they were in a fog. They sense a small hint of anger or a small hint of sadness, and it's very hard to reach that feeling. Workaholics often respond to queries about what they are feeling with a summary of what they are thinking.

5. Creating Crisis. The constant pressure and crisis with which workaholics choose to live creates excess adrenaline flow. Some workaholics report seeking this adrenaline high. Medical complications from repeated adrenaline highs may result in high blood pressure and increased stress on kidney and heart systems. All the medical problems associated with Type A personalities evolve into disease and death. Workaholics say they work better under pressure. This may be the only way in which the workaholic can get above numbness to any sense of feeling. Building crisis with work by taking on too much or working deadlines too close so I can work in a panic assures the adrenaline high and some sense of feeling. This "created" feeling comes from my fear of true feeling, of not being enough, or not being good enough. When I get into my compulsive doing I am using crisis

as a way to feel something and to escape what I really feel.

6. Isolation. Workaholics often isolate to the moment, into the movement, into the task and objects. This results in isolation, especially isolation away from ourselves and away from others. Workaholics have difficulty making personal contact with others. Workaholics have no friends, they have work associates and acquaintances. Both my brother and I are in this stage of our recovery process and have issues with making friends and making contact with others. We may look social on the surface, and we both avoid true intimacy.

7. Doing it all. Workaholics have difficulty letting others share in tasks. We often do the task before other workers or helpers are there, or we do the tasks after the workers have gone home. The housewife who complains that she cannot have a housekeeper help her work is into doing it all. Her addictive perfectionist behavior will expose her picking up the house for the housekeeper and redoing some of the rooms after the housekeeper has gone home. One of the ways workaholics con themselves into a fake level of wellness is to delegate tasks to employees, children or other victims. The workaholic spends even more energy figuring out not only what the "help" should do, but how and when they should do it. This adds to and protects the supply of work for the workaholic.

8. Boundaries. What is a boundary? A workaholic lacks boundaries. As a workaholic, I have difficulty knowing what tasks are mine to do and

what belongs to others. I may have difficulty letting other people have their feelings without flying into action. At the first sign of some emotion from others I may feel I have to comfort them or control them or to stop them. Having lack of boundaries for a workaholic is like a Vaudeville act of plate spinning. Workaholics spin their plates and others' plates too.

9. Using Stress Management as a band-aid. Workaholics use stress management to con themselves into a fake level of wellness. I have told myself if I lower the "stress" (effect of working too long and hard) I could handle "it". "It" is working crazy hours so I can stay in my disease.

10. Workaholics have a monotone mind. The workaholic cannot discuss or share with others experiences other than work and doing. We are not fun or pleasant to be with because we only talk enthusiastically about our jobs or other compulsive doing. Others may feel dizzy or bored after being with us.

11. Workaholics lack spontaneous playfulness. Workaholics participate in unplanned or unstructured play reluctantly, if at all. Play is for children, and workaholics have never been children. We are often adult children of dysfunctional or alcoholic families. Workaholics ruin vacations. It is not unusual for us to work on vacations or make vacation a task. Many workaholics may not even take vacations. If we play it is competitive and therefore becomes another task. Lack of spontaneity is the characteristic of workaholics that is especially debilitating to those in the arts or creative occupa-

tions. We are all in creative occupations at some level and we get so caught up in compulsion, in organizing ourselves and others, that our minds get constipated.

12. Late stage workaholics lack balance and may evidence extremes in behavior. They move between inexhaustible work and sitting so still they look like they are in a comatose state. Such a state is not recovery. Workaholics may evidence extremes of avoiding work or doing it all. They are paradoxically inefficient and costly to business and industry. Sometimes they may look like a procrastinator. A symptom of a need for recovery, procrastination is resentment of having to do the work.

13. Workaholics have preoccupation with constant thoughts of work. I have had several experiences with this, the most dangerous while driving. I have missed exists, arrived in another town much to my surprise, and had several near-hits with semis and cars. Workaholics can be found doing more than two things at once. For example, they may talk on the phone and answer mail or write checks.

14. Workaholics have tunnel vision. All attention is focused on tasks or objects. You may hear workaholics with this characteristic say, "Come hell or high water, I will get this done." This focus is very effective in freezing feelings. In later stages of workaholism tunnel vision is a literal phenomenon. I have experienced an actual narrowing of my vision field and have heard other workaholics speak of the same sensation. This becomes a safety problem. Some workaholics move at such speed in their tunnel vision phase they have no sense of their space in relationship

to their environment. Bruises and broken bones are often the results.

15. Packing. Workaholics often pack their schedules or pack things around wherever they go. I have been guilty of taking large cartons of files and paperwork on visits to my parents' home. I also have carted in my typewriter and my dictaphone. I have carted my stress-management tools and my gym clothes for my aerobics class that met three times a week to work with me. On the days the class did not meet, I carried my sneakers and running clothes because I ran on the off days or did exercises with the video tape in the office. I did this not from a need to keep healthy, but from a need not to hold still and feel.

16. "Homizing" the office. Workaholics often make their ofices look like home or like they would like their home to look in an effort to avoid going home. Home away from home. This becomes their domain and their area of control. They will go into the office on off times, out of a need for a fix.

17. Grandiosity. My belief as a workaholic is that I could do anything. If I don't know how I'll look it up in a book and do it. No job is too big or small for me to do alone. This characteristic also protects me from dependency on others and serves my disease by making me indispensable to others because of my know-how.

18. Workaholics, through their doing and jobs, are often dependent on other's dependency. I used other's dependency for my self-acknowledgement, my self-worth and my self-definition. I was employer.

17

I was consultant. I was counselor. Rather than be still and quiet enough to hear who I am, I would get into doing and believe that doing equaled importance and that importance equaled my existence. Self-worth came from my job.

19. Herd instinct. In order to validate our workaholism as acceptable we often join many professional clubs and organizations. Like the alcoholic who drinks in a bar with other buddies and compares his drinking to those around to con himself into a false sense of health, the work addict hangs around other workaholics to validate their disease as acceptable. We also use competition with our colleagues as a way to increase our disease.

20. Workaholics collect books or conferences. Workaholics often use external referenting to books or repeated attendance at various conferences to determine who they are. They look in the next book for the answer. They often prefer how-to, upward and onward type books to fiction. Many have not read fiction in years.

21. The phone. Workaholics often use the telephone like a straw to their supply. The phone connects them to their supply and validates who they are. It's not unusual to find the phone in their car as well as beside their beds at home. Workaholics may notice it is easier to talk over the phone to people than to talk to them in person. Some jobs enable workaholism by requiring employees to wear beepers. The workaholic likes others to hear their beepers go off. They feel important. Sometimes workaholics use

the mail to help them with their feeling of connection to people, places and things.

22. Burn-out is the bottom for the workaholic. Burn-out may present a subtle awareness that the office building doesn't suit you or as a desire to change departments or other subtle dissatisfaction. Burn-out may find expression in physical or mental illness. Just as the disease of alcoholism may end in death through suicide, body disease or mental illness, the same outcomes are available to the workaholic. I know a prominent physician who, after a few days of retirement, had a psychotic break and chose to stay in psychosis. He died within a year. His obituary was a glowing report of many accomplishments with the following predictive quote; "When I die I know God at the Pearly Gates will ask me what I have done for myself and I will have to tell Him I have done nothing." Another example of a relationship addict paradoxically avoiding true intimacy by using work with people as a fix.

Below is a space to list what you know about workaholism.

1.

2.

3.

4.

5.

LEARNING THE PROCESS OF WORK
ADDICTION

What is a nice girl like me doing with any addictions at all? God knows my parents did it right. They kept my brother and I warm, well-fed and clothed, in school, and in church and scouts. And further I lived in America, the land of promise. Focusing on that promise took my parents away from me and eventually me away from myself.

I have multiple addictions. I can use any person, place or thing addictively to stay away from my feelings and what I know. I notice I use absorbing focus on work (Workaholism, being in constant motion or doing) and losing myself in others' concerns (relationship addiction) and making illusions about others (romance addiction) as a distraction from the pain of my childhood. If those addictions are not active, I can substitute: food, alcohol, sex and spending money to escape that pain.

Most of us teach the process of addictive behavior to each other daily. I know I learned addictive behavior by watching many minute examples and demonstrations of addictive behavior patterns daily in my family, school, church and society. I learned most not to think for myself. I learned to be what my parents wanted me to be. I learned to conform and to

learn in the way my school taught me to learn and to
"do" religion the way my church instructed. I always
felt the adults in my life believed that I knew nothing
and that I had to be taught and molded. I *did* know.
I *knew* how I felt and no one asked, and if I said what
I felt anyway, no one listened. As a female child in the
late 1940s and early 1950s, I had very few models for
speaking my truth. I also knew as a child what I experienced and when I named that experience I was
sometimes punished for not being "nice."

Anne Wilson Schaef writes about the
characteristics of the addictive process in her books,
When Society Becomes the Addict and
Codependence Misunderstood-Mistreated. Using
these characteristics as a framework I became aware
of how I learned my addictive behavior early.

Parents are our first teachers and it is from my
parents that I learned a subtle and deadly form of
dishonesty. My parents were never in touch with their
feelings. My dad was not supposed to be in touch with
his feelings. A product of male socialization of the
early 1920s, he was a model rock and head of the
family. He was the good financial provider. Mom
may have felt her feelings at times and had no safe
way to express them. She was from the "children are
to be seen and not heard" era. As a female, she had
more permission to feel than dad did. Since Dad was
a workaholic, Mother had no audience. Eventually, she
too, disappeared into her doing and into her own
workaholism.

I learned early to smile big and say through my
teeth, that everything was OK. That's what my
parents did, and so did I. Can you picture the Dale

Carnegie smile? That is close to what I look like. Today my lined face reveals this old expression. I learned from my family, church, school and society to fill their expectations of who I was suppose to be without checking with myself about who I was. I was told to be a nice girl and that meant not naming what I saw or heard. I had to say nice things to people because not to do so would "hurt their feelings." I was taught over-responsibility (relationship addiction) by home and church. In my house, no one knew of people's responsibility for their own thoughts and feelings. I learned from this that control was outside of me. My feelings were "caused by others" not by how I talked to myself, and if others did not want me mad or sad they would be "nice" to me too. "Nice" used this way is a lie. I, as a human, did not exist. I was a daughter, a student and a sister. I was a Methodist in my Sunday uniform of Mary Janes and a Sunday dress. No one recognized, valued or supported my spirit (who I was and am at the core). Spirit was something one went to church for or about. Yet, there I learned nothing about spirituality. I learned religion.

I can still remember with a shiver what it felt like in my family when Mother was angry with Father and did not talk about it. And I also remember feeling responsible for it all. I learned from my mother how to express anger indirectly through illness, spending money and the use of food. We were well fed and often given sugared desserts. After any visit to a doctor or dentist, there was a treat in the form of ice cream or candy. A reward for pain. Little wonder that I now produce that pain through my workaholism and aerobic class before I can "reward" myself with a good meal, alcohol, a dessert or shopping. What a set up for addictive circling.

Impression management was big in our family. It was so big in our family that we pulled off the "Family of the Year" award at our church. The church was awarding "looking good" and "production", and my family did produce. Dad's business was successful, and he was in church every Sunday, and tithed regularly. By that time Mother had cared for many foster children. She always had one and sometimes two infants in her care. Focusing on children was the one way she escaped from her feelings. She often would say she had heard if one kept busy they would have no problems. Little did she know what she taught. As a family we looked good on the surface. The church was not aware of the isolation of the people in our home or of the silence there.

Gullibility is part of the dishonesty and part of what I learned. What could be more dishonest than believing almost anything I was told? I felt like Doris Day. Her characters believe most everything, and I did too. This trait made it easy for me to step across the line from gullibility to illusion-making. Illusion-making is a big part of my romanticizing my environment so it was comfortable. I conjured up images of myself as successful and desirable. I furthered my work addiction in this way. I learned to be gullible by watching my mother believe Dad's repeated promises of "I'll be home for dinner tonight by 6 p.m." and from their unquestioning manner around religious matters.

I bought into the promise as a child. I told

myself, "If only I'm a good little girl, Dad will come home to spend time with me. If only I study what they tell me, I can do anything they can do. If I am responsible and work hard, they will tell me they love me." My favorite promise from my parents was, "Let's do this job and be together." We were not together when we worked. We worked individually with little talk.

I learned nothing from church, school or home about trusting my own perceptions and my own gut reactions. I was not even aware I had a gut from which to catch a reaction, because I had numbed out my feelings. Numbing seemed like the way of life in my family. Both my parents did it. I rarely heard a feeling word; happy, sad, excited, angry, love. I grew up without hearing names of feelings or seeing them demonstrated or talked about. When upon occasion I could sense some feelings, I did not know what to call them or how to speak about feelings. I experienced much deadening and confusion.

Control is a major addictive characteristic in my family of origin. My dad is a master controller and demonstrated this in the family with his control of money and time. We all revolved around his workaholic time schedule, just as members of an alcoholic family revolve around the alcoholic.

Money use was decided by Dad. One of my memories is of a meeting my parents had on the budget. In this supposedly democratic meeting, I saw my mother upset, nervous and rigid. Her anger distorted to self-righteousness and occasional demands as she "met" with my father on money issues. I watched my mother become invisible. The truth was this was not a meeting of persons with common concern. My father was in the one-up, control position, and my mother sat one-down, a victim of her own thoughts during these meetings. I remember thinking, "No man will control me financially." This resolve also feeds my workaholism.

My mother controlled too, mostly with food and the use of sugar. From her I learned how to use substances to change feelings. Sugar kept us feeling subdued. I know she was not consciously aware of how sugar chemically affects the body, and I believe at some level she knew about the "satisfaction" that occured after we consumed a meal heavily doused with sugar. My dad would doze in his chair, and the rest of us would be off in our own sugar daze. Mom still hides sugar. Candy can be found in the dishcupboard, as well as the linen closet and clothing drawers. This is much like alcoholics who stash their supply of booze or workaholics who protect their supply of work. Mom now travels with her sugar supply, and always brings cookies, pies or sweet rolls with her on visits to my home.

Another characteristic of the addictive process was demonstrated daily by my school and church as well as home. Kindergarten through graduate years, I learned to look outside myself for other's approval and evaluation of my work. I had developed no way of evaluating my own effort other than by their criteria. Of course, in my workaholic home I learned you are your work and you are what you do. So, if I failed at school or any other production, that was a failure of me. I learned to take other's opinions and evaluations as the true reality, and only occasionally ask questions.

My patriarchal church taught me to look outside myself for all my religious needs and did nothing to aid my spiritual development. I learned a lot at church about who I was suppose to be. I learned how to further my relationship and romance addiction by serving others. The Good Christian Woman works hard and long, serving others in her church, home and community. In later years I used this church and home teaching to further my doing, to keep my calendar full and myself out of touch. I believed then the only way to be Christian was to work for and through the church. Church work was high on my list of things to do to look good, and by these doings I believed I was good. Why didn't I feel good? In church much was said about man being the head of the family and being a religious leader in his family. The implication I felt was that women could not do the same function. I further felt that my children and I were not a whole family if my spouse did not attend church. He did not attend church frequently, so I used my illusion-making and substituted other church men — the minister and occasionally God — as my "required" man. I pretended they were beside me in church and I got into my righteousness. This was a sick creation so I could meet the "requirements," of attendance as I illusioned them to be.

I also learned to measure my value by the use of the clock in my workaholic family. I learned that the more time spent in production, the more I was valued. I also learned to measure my worth by counting what I did. As children, I remember my brother and I had to carry so many bricks a day for our new house foundation, or had to weed so many rows of vegetables in the garden. I watched Mother leave out all the shirts that she had ironed during the day, her loaves of baked bread, and other products so Dad could see her *value* at the day's end.

Most of us teach addictive behavior to each other daily. Just as I learned my addictions through other's beliefs and behavior, I taught an addictive system to my children and reflected and modeled those behaviors to my peers.

BEING THE CHILD OF WORKAHOLIC PARENTS (Ghost Parents)

"All I remember is that I don't remember anything happening," said my brother reflectively as we sat discussing our early stories.

Prior to the age of five, I too had only a large void, a sense of loneliness and a feeling of abandonment for my earliest memories. I had memories of my dear grandmother rocking me by an open window. I remember little other nurturing physical contact.

Both my parents were workaholics. My father was the most extreme. His schedule of activity took him away in the early morning before I was up. He would often come home after my bed time at 8 p.m. or later and then I would hear him disappear into one of his many work projects. I still remember the feeling of loneliness when I would lay in my bed at night and see the outside lights reflecting on the lawn around dad's work area and hear his hammer pound on our house addition. I only remember seeing dad sit in his chair on Sunday afternoons. He would quickly fall asleep and be gone again. I did not have any memory of him when I was a small child. He simply was not there.

I remember him mostly as a stranger. Even when I did manage to get into his work schedule, he was not emotionally available to me. I experienced him to be a hollow, emotionally repressed man.

The only way I can remember relating to dad was through working his crazy work schedule. One of my earliest memories was all of us weeding the garden, in the dark, with the outside lights shining on the rows. My young fingers and mind had enough trouble distinguishing plants versus weeds in the daylight. I felt tired and confused and angry at this work and this way of relating with my father.

When I was twelve, I began to work with my father on Saturdays at his shop. We worked from 7:00 a.m. to 7:00 p.m. with 15 minutes for lunch. It was on the ride to and from work that I really noticed that I felt nonexistent and hurt with dad. He was totally preoccupied with work. He made lists while he was driving and talked on the car phone. He was generally in another space and not present with me. Abandoned again. Though I worked for many years on Saturdays, we were never able to take advantage of that travel time together to get to know each other.

My main parent was my workaholic and sometimes depressed mother. I know now her workaholism came out of her need to please others and do good. Thus, she was my main teacher of living in reaction to others (relationship addiction). Relationship addiction is another way of expressing the addictive process. Many authors name and write about this behavior as codependence. Melody Beattie, author of *Codependent No More* defined a codependent as a person who has let someone else's behavior affect him or her and who is obsessed with controlling other people's behavior. Anne Wilson Schaef, author of *Escape From Intimacy*, encourages her readers to drop the term codependence and name their relationship, romance and/or sexual addictions. The codependent can claim they are so named because of the significant addict in their life thus avoiding real program work on one's own addictions. She is right. I did this early in recovery.

I experienced abandonment with my mother. My earliest abandonment occured when I was in utero and immediately following my birth. My mother was depressed and suicidal during pregnancy. Both my parents were separately and silently grieving my deceased older sibling's death. He was still-born eleven months before my birth. Neither of my parents spoke about the death with each other nor spoke much about my coming birth. My mother did not consult her physician until her eighth month of pregnancy. She denied her pregnancy and me, as did my father.

Through much work in therapy and noticing of my feelings, I became aware of early memories in utero and the hostility of that environment. I wanted out and away from that place. I was delivered by Ceaserean section and in the early 1940s that meant that I was not wheeled into mother's room. Of course, fathers were not permitted to be with infants. My first two weeks, therefore, were spent in a bassinet in the hospital nursery. Mother had been heavily drugged for the procedure (in case I was also still-born). It took her days to come to and recover from her major surgery. We were separated by the institution and by the professional's lack of knowledge. The hospital's focus on mother's physical recovery completely ignored the emotional needs of both of us.

Childhood with a workaholic mother and father was like being a part-time child in a single-parent family. I remember much cleanliness, good meals and homemade clothing. I can still see mother's back to me as she stood working at the kitchen counters and doing her ironing. It is hard to crawl up on a lap when it is standing up or when it is filled with projects. I felt abandoned and lonely. The mixed message was, "I want to spend time with you, go away", for she often praised or bragged about me to others. She would dress me like a doll and curl my hair. I felt objectified and valued at the same time. I thought if she values me, she must want to spend time with me. Wrong. Hence the mixed message.

Evenings she sat with a lap full of knitting or other projects. No room for me. She often did two or three jobs at the same time. She hurried. Better stay out of the way, I thought. She was always doing things. Things and doing were more important than people and being with each other. In her relationship addiction my mother would try to make special things happen for my brother and me so we would not be disappointed about not having dad around. We made trips to the local soda fountain, to a friend's house or movies when he broke promises about coming home on time or promises about special activities. I learned play is used to erase pain.

Things did not improve as I grew and entered grade school. I participated in many programs and activities. I can still feel the disappointment and hurt I felt then when my father did not show up for my program or showed up for the last five or ten minutes and completely missed my part. This happened several times.

I don't know how my mother did it. Occasionally, it seemed as if mother made dad appear for picnics and even once for a six-week vacation. This is one of the few vacations I remember. During the vacation I clearly experienced living in the future and not the present moment. The whole vacation was an experience of tasks and measurements of time and distance and the goal of reaching destination by a specific time. I chose to ride up front with my dad, and my brother sat with my mother. I noticed dad was still not present. Many precious hours passed in the car when we could have shared and did not. My brother and I counted license plates and dead animals.

Our family did not talk much. If workaholic families convene at all it is occasionally around the dinner table. How can one feel left out at the dinner table with both parents present? It is easy. I remember sitting at the dinner table as a small child as Mom and Dad talked about the mechanics of running a home or talked about us children and did not talk to us. During my teen years we ate meals in silence in front of the television. I remember thinking, "Somebody talk to me!" "Where are you?!" As I write this I feel much pain and abandonment.

"Things" counted in our family. Mom used to say, "If it weren't for what I saved from the food budget, we wouldn't have anything." My brother and I did have things. On Christmas or birthdays we could not have taken away our presents until we had our pictures taken with them. Our things were displayed in collections or cataloged in scrapbooks. Our play area was always neat. Often our playthings were miniature work toys. We played at working.

The pain of loneliness in my workaholic family was more than loneliness. Although I had never been shunned as some religions practice, I experienced the pain of growing up in a workaholic family as a combination of loneliness and shunning, of not having the validation and the warm presence that human attention brings. I had ghost parents.

The family fun times (I can remember five) were something that was *done* and not an experience that was shared. The few family times that were intended to bring quality time to us were lost in a sea of days and years called nothingness. We were a family of strangers who did not know a language to share ourselves with each other. It is difficult to share oneself when you don't know who you are and what you are feeling. According to Anne Wilson Schaef this is the function of the addictive process, to keep us away from ourselves and our feelings.

Visits with my family after I left home continued to be painful; especially when I took along my controlling expectations of how I wanted my parents to be with me and how I wanted them to love me. Now, when I let go of these expectations and meet them where they are, I can notice myself and them and not miss who is not there. My pain comes from my own doing, from trying to control how they are for me.

What I notice now is our continuing difficulty with language and sharing. Attempting to share who I am with my non-recovering parents is painful and difficult. I do not feel safe sharing my feelings with them. I fear not being heard or being told I am not correct or having my feelings minimized by them. My father once attempted to control what I was sharing by telling me that I should not get too separate with my identity from my husband. We were discussing my work, hours and income. Work is the one topic we can speak about. Dad was upset when I spoke about *my* income and *my* business. His belief was that the business should also be my spouse's even though my spouse had nothing to do with that business.

My experience with my mother is that she longs for meaningful contact with anyone, as demonstrated by her many trips to the shopping centers to be among people. She manipulates to get anyone to engage in conversation by asking questions to which the answers are obvious. When that fails she begins comments which are descriptive of what is happening or descriptive of the surroundings — a type of monologue. She has only recently been able to name her loneliness in living with a spouse who does not speak with her. Perhaps she too is beginning her recovery.

CERTIFICATES, DIPLOMAS AND DEGREES

How many of these do I have to get before I know and can feel I am worth something? I feel scared at the recognition of my identity coming from being "professional." I am nonexistent.

Our society acknowledges transitions with certificates, degrees and diplomas from birth certificates to death certificates, Sunday school and Bible school certificates, Kindergarten to graduate-level diplomas. These, in fact, are more than acknowledgements. In our society they are used as measures of who we are, and they are used as goals toward which to work. By the time I had reached school age, I well understood these external measures and used them to define me. Like a horse wearing blinders, I went through the paces to get to the next diploma. The accompanying anticipation and anxiety often kept me focused in the future. With one degree under my belt I still felt "less than" and wondered why. I went on for the next degree and the next. Framed diplomas, certificates and awards filled my walls. Yet I was never enough. This was a familiar feeling.

It did not occur to me to follow my natural interest. Our high school guidance counselor met with each student in my high school class. "What did I want to do?", he asked. How would I know? I had not thought independently for years. "What did I want to be?", he prompted. Do I have to *do* to *be*, I wondered?

In my senior year I approached Mother with the idea that I wanted to go to college. "Let's ask your father", she responded. I got the feeling when talking with Dad that he had not saved for my future education. I was on my own to finance my way through school. The cycle of job and school equaled constant work.

EARLY SIGNS — BECOMING A WORKAHOLIC

From the very first day I loved grade school. I latched on to school in the absence of family. I tried to make school my family, and I moved into institutional unreality.

I still carry a vision of the first day. I see myself sitting on the wooden floor, happy, sitting apart from the other children, watching the dust particles in the sunbeam coming through the high windows. I can still smell the paste and ditto paper as I sat at the long, low table using the fat pencil. I was focused sharply and completely on marking my first test.

It is easy for me to recognize the beginnings of workaholism in the early grades. In second grade art class I remember being caught up in detail; I was driven by it. I was asked to draw a picture on the chalkboard and launched into a chalk drawing that included minute details and lasted well into recess. As I drew, the school room and my classmates disappeared. I got lost in the project. I felt good.

During the rest period when we had our heads on our desks, my little mind was running around about things to do.

In third grade I vividly remember Mrs. Crest and Margaret. Mrs. Crest was beautiful and I felt special around her. Mrs. Crest believed in herself. I somehow used that to validate me. She used to brush my hair and braid it after playground period. I worked for her. I knew she believed in me, and with that to hold on to I also believed in me. I kept my desk straight, compulsively so, for desk inspection. My cigar box filled with pencils, erasers, and sharpener was impeccable. My papers were in order. I tried very hard for her and felt the pat on the head — my first fix. Many times afterward I sought that fix.

Margaret was my best friend. She was a slender blonde with expensive clothing. Margaret was often sick, and I helped when she threw-up by getting a cold cloth for her head or by walking her to the nurse's office. I had become a helper at age eight. Mrs. Crest and Margaret used to call me "nurse." I puffed up with my new label. I watched Margaret often for signs that she would be ill so I could go into action. I ran into a double bind. If I watched and worried about her, I missed the lesson and my pat on the head for performance. She didn't throw-up enough. I had to make a choice. Little did I know that Mrs. Crest and Margaret had correctly spotted and were identifying my budding relationship addiction and workaholism. They knew not what they named. Neither did they realize how they were using and influencing me.

In junior high school, my workaholism and romance addiction literally landed me in a hole. Our class was going to the library to write our research papers. I had double research to do as I was secretly writing two papers; mine and my new boyfriend's. Our junior high building was separate from the high school, and we shared the high school library. A deep ditch had been dug between the buildings for sewer repair and was crossable by a wide plank. I was in love with Russell and I constantly looked for him to see if he noticed me. Crossing the plank safely proved impossible when I spotted him in the line behind me. I crashed down into the eight-foot hole, pulled all of the muscles in my back and cut and scraped myself. The fall did not knock any sense into me. I still did not realize what had happened. When I returned to school, I used the "crisis" to be special and become the center of attention.

I remember disappearing into my bedroom a lot during my teen years to escape into compulsive list making. I would compulsively organize my clothing and make lists of different combinations. I once had a roommate after college graduation who did an advanced form of my behavior. On a large calendar she wrote each day's outfit, shoes and accessories. She made these wardrobe plans for three months in advance. This took up lots of time and was the beginning of many list making sessions.

During college my all night study binges were workaholic. I really started getting into time structuring when my fraternal organization elected me pledge trainer. I balanced the responsibility of thirty pledges on top of my study load. That same year I added a part in the college play which extended my day as a commuting student into numbness. I felt in control and on top of the world in my workaholism. However, being in control is not a feeling. What I was experiencing was my first adrenaline rush, and I maintained that adrenaline with constant activity.

It was during undergraduate years that I began using caffeine to maintain my adrenaline high. Alcohol followed to help me slow down and sleep.

This was the beginning of my addictive use of these substances.

The awards began to come at this time. I was selected by a professor to teach his classes during his absence. My fraternity rewarded me for my leadership with a dinner, a memory book and a silver bracelet. It was like receiving the proverbial gold watch at twenty-one. I was surprised that I felt detached and hollow at receiving this recognition and the awards. I was cut off from the joy of the celebration. I got my fix in the compulsive doing not the flourishes at the end. By my senior year, I was constantly looking for the next project and a way to "protect my supply" of projects. I am borrowing the term "protect supply" from alcoholics who protect their supply of alcohol by hiding bottles. Workaholics proudly expose their supply. I did not hide my work addiction and supply of projects. I got some hollow resemblance of intimacy when I spoke with others about my project list. Since I had not experienced intimacy in my family it was easy to mistake simple attentiveness or passing interest for intimacy. I needed to feel central, on stage. I needed to perform and receive the adulation of those around me. Why did I not trust what I received, and why did I seek more?

Moving out of my home after college I felt driven to do an excellent job and do it all. I moved into my first apartment at the beginning of the summer. I had obtained a teaching position at a nearby school for that fall. I spent a busy summer decorating my apartment, making lesson plans, visiting the school and arranging and rearranging the room and the bulletin boards.

As I began my first work assignment, I would spend hours planning lessons, inventing displays and numbing out. It was not normal for a twenty-two-year-old to spend Friday night doing paper work. I had lost my ability to play long ago. I got into impression management — trying to control other's impressions of me by what I had worn and how I acted. I was a walking, self-righteous advertisement.

I began spending time pursuing a man. Marriage was supposed to be next. This was the 1960s and I did not consider the other alternatives. This was simply what was next on the list. I compulsively followed society's agenda. And I succeeded through dishonesty and manipulation to land my husband eight months later.

After a honeymoon night in a hotel in Louisville, we headed to our new hometown. Washington Street in Indianapolis was bleak. I remember the feeling of slipping into a role that was familiar, a role I had once seen my mother take with Dad. Though familiar, it was heavy and smothering. We located our first apartment, a beautiful old structure on North Meridian Street. The first thing I did? Decorate? No, I got a job. With only six weeks left in the public school year I looked for and got a temporary job at Arsenal Tech High School. There was Doris Day again, teaching at an inner-city school knowing nothing about inner-city children or safety. I was taking knives away from students and making sure all my students had books for the last six weeks even though many of them could not read. I was acting "as if." As if I had control, answers and power which was quite a fix for someone who felt at some level she had no control. I was beginning to notice my addictive process and compulsive work.

In the early weeks of being married to Bill I became painfully aware I did not know a thing about relationships or how to be in a relationship. I was using my mother's way of relating to a husband. I completely centered myself around Bill's needs, his schedule, his doings and his depression. I buried myself in menu planning. I could lose myself for hours in this task. I balanced meals. I balanced the weeks' intake of food. I made menus for each day of the week, each meal of the day. I fixed very elaborate dishes. I had developed a relationship with my kitchen. What a fix! I got a feeling of being in control and of being in power from those hours. It was also my long distance way of relating to my husband.

One Saturday morning after we had settled in, I was standing at the third story kitchen window doing the dishes and watching Bill as he tinkered with his car below. I was aware of Saturday in that moment. I was aware of a great expanse of time and began wondering what "we" would do today. I felt lost as I waited for Bill to finish the car repair. I had nothing to do. I had, in my workaholic state, come to the place workaholic persons fear. I had not protected my supply of work.

I went down the back stairs of the apartment building and asked Bill what we were going to do today. Four weeks into the marriage and I had no idea what I wanted to do or needed. I asked my husband for that information. The clues were getting bigger, and I still did not notice.

Silence was frightening to me when it occured

44

between us. I remember early in the marriage sitting with Bill and having nothing to say to him and he having nothing to say to me. So I made up nonsense songs to sing or I would tease him to get a reaction. I sensed his depression and I felt responsible. I needed to fix it. Hadn't I done this another time? Mother. Yes I had. I was also beginning to feel the abandonment of being with a person who is depressed and being with a person who is not there emotionally.

Sex was another matter. I knew sex was a part of my role as a wife and I also knew sex was dirty. This was information from my mother, Dad and my experiences with church and society.

I started my period at age twelve and with it came sexual molestation. Although repeated molestings did not occur, sexual harassment from this distant male relative did occur for the next two years. I was enraged at my mother, father and other relatives who did not notice him pinching my breasts and feeling my legs or bottom. He loved sneaking in their presence, apparently succeeding in the game by not getting caught. I reacted by avoiding and withdrawing. Sex was an unmentionable in my emotionally repressed family, and I could not tell anyone.

I remember one day asking mother if she needed to tell me anything about sex. Her response was to look down at the floor and say nothing. In the absence of information, my mind raced into thinking it was awful, terrible and dirty. It was years later during recovery, that I risked speaking to my mother about the sexual molestation. I felt compelled to speak with her about my knowings. She was not shocked as I shared with her what had happened to me. The sexual and emotional repression was so severe, that my mother and I did not speak about the incident until 30 years later. It wasn't until then that my process and recovery afforded me the maturity to do so.

I had noticed that Bill and I had a different pace. My pace was fast, action-oriented, and on the move. His pace was somewhere between laid-back and asleep, and he did lots of sleep. I disappeared for long periods of time into activity trying to avoid the intimacy which I feared. If I really had looked, I would have noticed he wasn't there. I had married a workaholic who slept a lot when he was home. In place of this relationship, I made an illusion of intimacy and an illusion of closeness. The truth was I did not know this man *and* I knew him at the same time. I had only a total of ten dates and one summer of experience with him. I knew his father was an alcoholic and did not know the meaning this would have for me. I sensed and knew well the parts of him that were chronically depressed, distant and not present. These parts were very much like my mother. So I made the rest of him up. I made up our relationship and kept my distance.

MARRIAGE AS A WORKAHOLIC

Me, married to a workaholic? No problem. None, as long as I am compulsive with working too. . . until the noticing begins.

I did not notice my husband's being gone, and when I did notice, I simply continued my illusionary relationship with him. I saw him as the volatile, sensitive artist, who needed me because he was depressed. And I needed his needing me. I needed to focus on his depression as a part of my relationship addiction. As part of my workaholism, I could stay busy trying to cheer him up, and be responsible for his expression of feeling with his children and his relatives. My business was to block my abandonment feelings and my sadness which crept in when I slowed my own work pace and began to feel. I also wanted to block my feelings around the reality of what it was like to live with someone who is constantly negative and perfectionistic.

My focus on his illness grew into resentment. My control illusions grew too. I resented his depression and workaholism. Mostly I resented my constant focus on his problem.

It was becoming harder to do it all. I functioned as if I was responsible for the total relationship. In my unrecovery around my sexual issues, I manipulated the infrequency of our sexual contact and blamed it on him. I volunteered to do the bills and bookkeeping out of my need to control the money and my need to take care of his depression. I conned myself: if I took this task off his shoulders, he would be less depressed. I did not tell myself about my own work addiction.

The children never had a chance to get close to their father. I was in charge. Their schedule was mine. Discipline was mine. I could relieve his stress I told myself. I felt indispensable, needed and central. I could also keep very busy.

With all this responsibility came the one-up move. I must be superior, brighter and stronger if I can do all this. Poor weak man. Where had I learned to confuse love and pity? Echoes of a Good Christian Woman. Echoes of my mother's sigh.

Occasionally I would imagine relationships with other men. I have since learned this was my romance addiction in action. I thought those relationships were my secret. I was not aware my thoughts were showing through as seductive behavior with these men.

What I know now is I had no knowledge about relationships or being in them. I did not trust men. My father had abandoned me, a distant male relative had sexually abused me, the men in the church preached how to control me and men teachers taught me not to get too smart. Allowing myself to get close in a relationship with a male meant being open to control and more abandonment pain.

My trust issues included women. I could rationalize historically my lack of caring and connectedness to men. I had a difficult time explaining away my lack of trust with women. I felt betrayed by my own kind. The dualistic separation of trust issues with men and women is one of the characteristics of my disease. They are one in the same: basic fear of emotional pain. I had a belief that I was unworthy and no good and would be abandoned.

It did not occur to me until I was two years into recovery work that healthy relationships live, move and breathe. A relationship is not something one does. A relationship is something that occurs between two or more people when they share who they honestly are and what they notice with each other.

My rush to get pregnant after my marriage was from my workaholism and my hope that I would not be approached for sex often as I grew in size. I also thought that was the next thing I was supposed to do as a wife. My complete detachment around sex gave me no clue of my sexual problems. I had no awareness of myself sexually other than my horrible incest experience. I objectified myself and Bill into roles as husband and wife sexually to avoid working through my pain around the incest. I know today much of my compulsive doing and work was also meant to hold off my feelings about the sexual molesting.

From the beginning in our marriage I had always used alcohol when I was having sex. I did not know what it was like to have sex when I was not using alcohol.

I knew a lot about seduction. Strangely, seduction was something I used mostly with other men and sometimes with my husband. In preparation for my marriage I had sewn a whole wardrobe of seductive nightwear. These felt like costumes as I wore them, and they were costumes for another fantasy. I had sex with that part of myself that had been molested and harassed. My other sexual feelings were repressed and held down with all the strength and illusion of control I could muster. The alcohol helped too. These repressed sexual feelings would be dangerous to let out, I believed.

Soon after I became pregnant I began living in the future with thoughts of the baby's needs. I worked for hours on the child's room, clothes and toys. I read books on child care and child development. I was going to do this right (perfect), and I was scared. Waves of fear hit me when I would think of child birth and of motherhood. Child care held no fear for me. I had that part down pat from my childhood experience of living with and caring for over one hundred foster care children in my mother's home. My fears were about the emptiness I felt when I was increasingly busy with a pregnancy. How can one be pregnant and feel empty? I did. I was moving even further away from myself.

Bill and I did childbirth class together and I still felt alone. I was alone. I had completely left myself. Self-abandonment is the worst form of abandonment. It is self abuse.

WORKAHOLISM — FULL-BLOWN

Motherhood was quite a facilitator of my addictive process as expressed through my workaholism and relationship addiction. I followed old patterns of giving all to the children.

Just after the birth of my son, I immediately organized myself totally around his needs and schedule. I'm not writing here about the normal amount of caretaking that goes into childcare of infants. I'm writing about my compulsiveness and the resulting self-neglect.

My connection the first six weeks through breast feeding was a reality. My child needed me. Now here was the opposite of the abandonment feeling. What magic. From that abandonment cure I moved to centering myself around this child's needs way past the time when that was healthy for him or for me. I was so focused on my child that I did not want to go out with my husband. I spent our first date away thinking of my baby and his needs. I missed being present in the moment with my husband and missed the movie we were watching. I experienced this date as intrusive into the mother-son relationship.

The days seemed to be an endless cycle of unfinished tasks from feeding, bathing, dressing, rocking, laundering and brief contact with my husband.

51

My caffeine intake increased. I was still missing myself. My answer to this feeling of emptiness was to begin my master's level study at a nearby university when my child was eight weeks old. I remember beginning to objectify my child at that point by feeding him a bottle while reading my textbook and becoming very functional with him about his care. I certainly was not emotionally available to him and provided his first abandonment experience. This was not something a mother willingly enters into a child's baby book!

I felt the physical tiredness that was there after childbirth, and now I pushed myself through it. To sit and give in and be with the tiredness meant I could not get my fix from doing and workaholism. Now, I told myself, I had to take care of two persons. I did not realize that I also objectified and began at that time to clearly treat Bill as a child and saw myself as his mother. How could a woman have sex with her child? It was another reason not to be present with my husband during sex.

The following years were full of being a super mom and doing it right. We moved twice, I completed a master's degree, and I gave birth to my daughter.

It was now easy to get my adrenaline high. One particular Saturday morning, Pat and John, our neighbors, visited our house around 9:30. I had been up since 6:00 a.m., baked bread, painted the kitchen cabinets, dressed the children and had them involved somewhere. As Pat and John sat at our kitchen table, John remarked about my nervous energy. I realized then I was literally shaking and heard myself running off at the mouth. In conversation with them I was asking double questions and answering them before they had a chance. John and Pat didn't stay long that day. I am grateful John noticed and called attention to my behavior.

My compulsive list making reached an all time high one day when I ran out of paper on which to write. I reached for a magic marker and on each pane of the kitchen window listed a day of the week and each day's activities. People were not on the list. I felt embarrassed and angry when Bill told me my crazy window list was to be erased. I knew he was right. There was something crazy about what I had done.

My isolation increased during early family years. I had contact with few friends because I had only a scattered few and had not taken time to invest in the relationships. I did not know how to have relationships. All of my relationships at home and the univeristy were centered around work. I did not know how to relate by just being myself.

My compulsive efforts not to feel began extending to my food. I began counting calories, amounts and began restricting my food. I felt powerful when I controlled my food. How could I be so out of control with workaholism and con myself with control around food? I felt very successful with my food control as evidenced by my smallness. I used magazines to further my list making. Talk about external referenting! Every month I would buy *Woman's Day, Better Homes and Garden, Ladies Home Journal,* and several other magazines to give me ideas. I kept my time schedule racing full steam ahead with these new tasks. Don't feel, don't feel, don't feel me.

When my daughter neared her first birthday, I

began to think about going back to work full-time. I let myself know I missed contacts with adults. Through months of repetition I thought I had perfected housekeeping and child rearing. Tasks took up less and less of my time. How could I fill more time?

I found a full-time position at a nearby high school and found myself ambivalent about returning to work. No one could do the mom job like I had perfected it in my illusionary world. A long stream of babysitters followed. I disappeared even further into doing. I performed on the job not for the paycheck or even self-esteem as much as for the motion and task fix so I could remain emotionally dead. What might I have felt if I stopped long enough to feel? I might have felt my repressed feelings about past abandonments. I might also have felt anger about being objectified by my workaholic parents. I might have felt the anger about the incest and sexual harassment. I surely would have felt the anger about church and school's focus on thinking about others first when I was so needy. Emotionally I was an infant. All this emotional detachment is not to say I did not feel love for my children. I did, though it felt misty and distant.

I worked as a high school teacher in the business department teaching typing and general business. My need for an adrenaline high and crisis was easily accomplished there.

Teachers usually complain if they have to prepare for more than four classes. I organized my classes so I had 25 preparations for *each* class by giving each student a choice on how to do the assignment. The classroom looked like a circus as some students used art to do the unit, some worked with tape recorders, books, typewriters, films and lecture. I further extended the grading task by writing long notes to students and parents to externally reward their efforts. I worked seven days a week on lesson preparation and grading. I functioned as part of the addictive system modeling it for students by providing external rewards, using perfectionism to further student's inadequacy and my superiority, and requiring student obedience. I had to control. My controlling behavior gave me a false sense of power, and I knew nothing about personal power. I illusioned I had power over others.

My numbness continued as I moved into school counseling following my master's work. School counseling in the early 1960s was emerging from a background of advising a few college-bound students on programs and school to the 1970s which included personal growth. This was something I also needed for myself.

I began to notice my numbness and tiredness in my job as school counselor. Of course I was tired. Unwilling to accept the job as student advisor, I began designing elaborate programs and units for students to aid their personal growth (and mine) in a sick system. All the while I continued my compulsive disappearance into doing and workaholism.

I recognized something was wrong when I heard myself say out loud, "What do I have to do to get a rest? Get sick?" Three months later I did enter the hospital for an operation on a benign cyst and got some of the rest needed. I allowed it was permissible to rest in illness only. This was a behavior I had seen my mother do repeatedly. After being released from the hospital I continued to notice my tiredness and my feeling that I was not healthy. I know now this was my first step toward recovery.

STOP THE WORLD I WANT TO GET OFF

"Sounds like you're missing yourself," Anne said as tears ran down my face. I sobbed. I was filled with a strange hot feeling in the middle of a cold room in Deerwood, Minnesota. It was November and I was at my first Living Process Intensive with Anne Wilson Schaef.

I had begun introducing myself to the group and in typical workaholic fashion listed all the things I was doing. I named my various work projects, job, committees, community work and self-imposed running and stress-management program. And as I did I heard my voice rise and get angry. "I am tired", I let myself and the group know.

Anne's comment about missing myself rang so true. Deep from within, my grief emerged and rose to the surface. The others in the group sat waiting while I cried. I thought the group was hating me because I was taking so much time from them.

Anne directed my awareness toward my arms and my rigid hands and fingers. I noticed and shifted. Then I was gone from the room. The participants faded into the background as I faded into my core, a place I hadn't been in some 30 years. I felt an overwhelming fear and sadness there, and I knew this part of me and part of my past experience. I didn't know what these feelings were about. I continued crying.

I could feel my body shift to center and my muscles relax as I breathed into my core. A gentle warm flood followed. I was aware for the first time that I liked me. Until that moment I had not held still enough to know me. I laughed and I heard the group laugh. I was so amused to know simply I liked me. That was several years ago and the power and impact of that moment has remained with me as if it were as important a moment as my birth. And it was.

My awareness shifted from my core back to the group and the room. I sensed my living. Anne invited me to share with the group what I knew. As I did, I heard my clarity. I told them I had thought at first the group was thinking hurry up. And, I told them, I knew that was me thinking hurry up. I knew this was from living with hurried parents. I shared with them my knowing about liking me.

The group responded with their own experiences as they watched me stay with myself and my feelings. "Powerful, spiritual, frightening," they told me. I felt amazed at their comments. I was amazed at myself, and I knew there was more to come. I spent a lot of time that week with myself. That's what you do when you like someone. I also was able to spend time with others in the group. Many of them were really present, and that was a new experience for me. I was used to bodies where spirits were gone because people were absorbed in their work, in television and in the newspaper. I was having an amazing experience in real living by being with people who looked at me when we talked, people who spoke about their feelings, and people who knew who they really were and shared it. I had rarely experienced this in my world. I noticed the abandonment feeling was not as painful when I was present with myself and they were present with me. The intensive was a healing experience for me and I wanted more. I knew I had to go home to my own doings, a crazy and self-imposed work schedule, family over-responsibility, community work and my workaholic husband. I did not want to go home. This was another nudge toward recovery.

In that week I heard others share and do their own deep process work. I began learning about addiction and how we use addictions to stay away from ourselves. Anne Wilson Schaef writes in her book *Co-dependence Misunderstood-Mistreated* that addictions are processes over which we are powerless. These addictions keep us unaware of feelings and knowings so we don't have to take responsibility for ourselves. We lie to ourselves and to others, and part of our recovery is becoming willing to give up this process. The book *Co-dependence Misunderstood-Mistreated* had not been written when I was at Deerwood so I experienced part of the book in its oral beginning as Anne and others spoke about their addictions and their personal stories. Many spoke of step work and twelve-step programs like Alcoholics Anonymous, Overeaters Anonymous and Alanon.

I heard from other women the importance of knowing and acknowledging their stories and their experiences as they grew up. I had few early childhood memories of events and even less memory of any feelings I had had as a child. The search began. I was open to knowing my childhood experiences. The memories did not come flooding in. I looked through old photo albums searching the faces and the expressions. I spoke to members of my family about early family history. My brother and I told each other our stories one special summer day. I read journals and diaries from my mother and grandmother. Memories and knowings came slowly in spite of my workaholic attack on my own history. Most memories came when I sat quietly and listened to myself. Sometimes information came through following feelings I experienced.

THE PROCESS OF THE DISEASE OF
WORKAHOLISM AND RECOVERY

The process of my disease of workaholism moves from thoughts to behaviors to numbness to repetitive doing. The process of my recovery moves through the disease from my center out. It moves from a vague awareness that I am in a rut (a grave with open ends) through the numbness and behaviors and through my thoughts. Orders from myself or others to produce or manifest flow into thoughts of my production, not being good enough, into shame and rage and anger. I began isolating. I isolate into the pain and begin doing it all myself (control). Schaef writes about ingestive addictions as those substances; alcohol, drugs, food, sugar, caffeine, nicotine; we consume to numb out. Process addictions are processes used to numb out: work, amassing money or spending money, sex and gambling. I move between ingestive and process addictions in my disease process. When one does not work, I try another.

Feeling any feeling can be an invitation into my disease. I was taught to fear feelings. Feelings were so taboo they were not talked about at home, school or church. So feeling a hint of anything triggers me into my need to be in control and into my addictive process. I particularly did not want to have anything to do with my old feeling of abandonment and abuse.

61

My relationship addiction is an avenue into my workaholism and directly related to the adult child of alcoholic characteristic of "I don't know what I feel. I know what you feel and what you want." As the workaholic I added "and I must provide it for you." My illusion-making is an invitation into my disease. I tell myself the cliche "the world is what I make it" and become busy creating the illusion and this gets me into my workaholism.

Assumptions about what you want me to do or be lead me to list making and tasks. In my disease of workaholism I never check out my assumptions with you. I use these assumptions to make my list. I use my assumptions about your needs to pad my own do list and assure my supply of things to do.

Feeling resentment is a sign of my bottoming out. When I began to resent calls from people wanting appointments, other people's requests, etc., I know I have overindulged them and am into compulsive doing and work. I feel heavy. Building tolerance to work becomes part of the disease process. Forty hours becomes sixty hours becomes eighty hours. Rather than be honest about not knowing who I am, that I am, I compulsively up the anty of hours.

Using the illusion of control that comes from compulsive movement and work, I protect myself from feeling fear and abandonment. I would tap into the abandonment pain often being married to a workaholic and working with and being around non-recovering people. I did not want to feel the fear I had around sex as an incest survivor. I know nothing during the process of my disease about my ability to respond to my own pain and my environment. Ironically, this is self-abuse, a lack of self-protection.

I suspect my workaholism is also self-stimulation. I was a cesarean section delivery and in the 1940s it was not procedure to stimulate these infants. My early life was void of much stimulation and social interaction from parents who were not emotionally present and isolated into their own disease process. One early awareness I had of myself was propelling myself as soon as I could into activity. I am now beginning to not push as I notice who I am.

The process of my recovery involves moving through myself into self-care, self-knowing and self-responding. This is not self-centeredness. Whitfield also writes about this process in his book *Healing the Child Within*.

I am coming to know work as an expression of myself. Work in recovery lacks the characteristics of the disease and is hard to distinguish from play. It is not heavy. It is light and often lacks form. I am learning that living is a process not a product.

It is not unusual to uncover multiple addictions as one begins recovery and this is exactly what happened to me. I was sharing with my Thursday group and I noted a slip in the use of terms as I told them "How can I write a chapter on recovery from workaholism using the steps when I have not done individual work with a sponsor around my alcohol. . . I mean workaholism." I was surprised to hear myself say this as I had finished a 12-step workshop around my workaholism. The workshop had taken over a year to complete. Yet that slip was important and I took notice.

63

MOVING FROM THE INSIDE OUT

For three years I had been flowing through different awarenesses about myself and alcohol as I started recovery around workaholic and relationship issues. I had owned that I had used alcohol addictively which is true. And another level of honesty is to say I am alcoholic. The first sounds rather clinical which is a clue in itself. One of my addictive patterns is to study the subject, run myself through some kind of checklist quite similar to popular magazine checklists and then label myself accordingly. I believe this is a move into my denial and a way of objectifying and abusing myself. My checklist habit comes out of not knowing who I am and wanting to label myself. Doing step work around alcohol is different and the same as doing it around my workaholism and I seem to be approaching them simultaneously. I have heard it said as an alcoholic recovers he or she is likely to find their relationship addiction (called codependence by some authors) under their alcoholism. It is not surprising to me that after three years of recovery work around my codependence I find my alcoholism without bottoming out. I am grateful I could identify the addiction before it cost me more than it had already.

Knowing I was open and ready, I sought out a woman who had several years sobriety with alcohol and spent time telling her about my "low-grade, every now and then use". She was wonderfully patient with me and kept bringing me back to the question "What happens when you use?" "Does or has alcohol caused a problem for you?" She did not ask why do you drink or how much or when but *what* happens.

My answer to "what", involved me in discovering my physical, spiritual and intellectual symptoms which clearly told me alcohol was a problem. The same knowing occurs with work addiction though harder to come by because workaholism is so highly reinforced by our society. What happens to me when I work addictively affects me physically, spiritually, intellectually and socially. Whether alcohol or work, the purpose of my addictive use is not to feel. I do addictions sometimes to avoid good and pleasant feelings as well as pain.

When I use work as a fix, I numb out and push myself past tired into physical exhaustion where it is difficult to work safely. I become blurry eyed. My stress level runs high. Stress is a nice denial word for workaholism and other addictive behaviors. My skin reacts with increased dandruff and seborrhea as well as other rashes. People have different physiological systems with which they respond to stress. My vulnerable physiological system seems to be my skin. It becomes diffucult for me to sleep. My body aches for rest and my mind won't shut-up, or my body hurts from too much physical work, or at times from too much sitting and not enough physical work. My stomach reacts with excess acid and my breath turns sour. I urinate more frequently. If I come down with a cold, flu or diarrhea, I often would not suspect my body's need for rest and work through my illness never missing a day.

Intellectually my mind eludes me into grandiose control. "I'm really doing it all." "All it takes is effort." "I can do most anything I want." All of which takes me away from respecting who I am in the moment. I get into my illusion of a professional, efficient machine who is loved by, important to, central and one-up to everyone. In my illusion and complusive thinking I often double schedule and misplace papers or have blackouts about important tasks or dates.

Does workaholism cause me a problem? YES! When I am into workaholism, I am not spiritual. I do not exist. I am my work. (I am not writing about religion. In the height of my workaholism I attended church quite regularly. Religion was another job on my list. This was something to do and not about being.)

I have big problems with boundaries when I am into my workaholism. I don't know where I stop and others start. I have trouble saying "no" to more work or to being used by other addictive persons. I cannot take care of and protect myself from use and abuse.

Workaholism causes me a problem with relationships. I remain isolated and underdeveloped socially. I have no friends and my only acquaintances are from the workplace. I know nothing about sharing myself with others as I do not perceive a self to share. I feel bored and avoid social functions which are not for business.

All these spiral me further into my addiction and away from being and feeling. Has workaholism ever caused me a problem in my primary relationship?

Yes! I have used work addiction to avoid all facets of the relationship. Being a workaholic married to a workaholic is like having a drinking buddy. "You're working late? Me too! See you at 10:00 p.m.", guaranteed a safe relationship distance, avoidance of identifying issues between us and a zombie partnership. Terry Kellogg, psychotherapist and lecturer, uses the term "human doings" to describe people who are into workaholism. Two "human doings" under the same roof describes two workaholics in a relationship.

I have done extensive step work around my relationship addiction. I know at many different levels I also was working through steps on my other addictions. Removing a few bricks in a wall will weaken the wall; likewise, working the steps around one addiction weakens other addictions. This is a process I will often repeat as new information comes to me on how I avoid feelings and being human. It is important to attend twelve-step meetings specific to each addiction and to let the group and their talk help chip away at the denial that is part of each addict's life.

Relationship ignorance underlies all addictions. We do not know how to relate in a healthy way with ourselves or others. Alanon is a good place for the addict to learn about boundaries and detachment. A.C.O.A. (Adult Children of Alcoholics) is a place to begin work about early childhood memories and pain. This group gives permission to feel. It is important to work through both of these groups. Remember, there is a lot of time.

As a workaholic I valued order, logic and lists and had preconceived ideas about recovery and progression of recovery. Of course I did not, as a workaholic, acknowledge recovery as a process. I thought it was a task, once accomplished, that could be put to rest.

What I know about my recovery is that it is gentle, respectful and it takes time. I suspect there is no one pattern or right way for recovery. That is new. No list from a master list maker!

Everything that has happened to me has been part of my recovery, even my abandonment, abuse and ensuing addictions. Without the addictions there would have been no recovery. My own recovery has taken form and direction through simply noticing, journalizing, counseling with professionals, twelve-step programs and prayer and meditation. The year I spent with twelve women in Indianapolis in a twelve-step workshop also facilitated my recovery process. Doing step-work, mid-day, mid-week with other women with various addictions helped me get in touch with how I substitute addictions. I believe it is important to name my major addictions and to know and understand secondary addictions which trail after. One level of my denial was a blanket statement that I had an addictive personality. Again true and not honest, for there is more to let myself know and name than meets the eye. Part of my responsibility to me is to name, know, accept and seek recovery around each addiction.

What is key is *willingness* to give up old behaviors and face unstructured time. This allows me to begin to notice how workaholism and doing affects the quality of my life. In being willing to face unstructured time, I listen more to myself and my knowing about what I want to do rather than what I am supposed to do to meet other's expectations. The result is not chaos. The result is flow. The result is me opening to my spirituality. It is terrifying and unlikely that the workaholic will provide an unstructured space of time for her recovery. My willingness to experience unstructured time did not come through my own generosity and self-caring. I lost a major consulting contract which cut my work week hours back to a human pace. I considered beating the bushes to generate work to replace the lost contract hours (illusion of control). These thoughts did not last long for by that time I had six months experience with Living Process Groups. The time spent with Living Process Groups experiencing a different way of being proved a crucial facilitator in my recovery from workaholism. It was during these groups that I allowed the detoxifying experience of unplanned time. During this time, without my fix from compulsive doing and work, my long repressed and unidentified feelings began to surface. I was supported by those present in allowing these feelings to surface. I was encouraged to name feelings myself and to understand the information brought by my emerging feelings. My terror came from my assumption that feelings would rush to the surface at the same speedy pace I moved in my workaholism. Recovery of myself began. When I was still enough and quiet I could hear what I needed to know in that moment. Learning to trust this process is important and central to my recovery.

What is also key is my noticing and that noticing comes from my inside out. Recovery does not come through external tasks, check lists or professional wisdom; although, these may provide triggers for internal or external noticings. I am aware how many living things in the universe develop from the inside out; earth, vegetation, seeds and babies. Developing from the inside out may be one of the holograms of the universe.

A central learning in my recovery process is that I did not have to do it alone. As a child of a dysfunctional, emotionally repressed family, I vowed early to do things myself. I could count on me to do. Learning I needed to use a counselor, a twelve-step program, others in the program, and a sponsor for my recovery was slowly accepted. I had big trust issues.

I spent a year in training with Anne Wilson Schaef as part of my recovery. That year was an important catalyst. I approached the training as a way to augment my workaholism. I told myself I was in training for my clients so I could be a better therapist. I was really in training to block out more time from home so I would not feel the pain of me in my relationships. I took the training bibliography seriously. I read and crossed off books as I conquered them. I did meditative reading compulsively sometimes carrying around up to four books at a time. I would not miss a monthly weekend meeting with other trainees in my geographic area or a twelve-step meeting. This was from my need to block out my time and feelings, not from the need for or the commitment to a program of recovery. I was very good at conning myself. I later came to know the importance of checking my motives.

By dualistically setting up "the other side", which was any experience or setting outside the training group, I made the gulf between my experiences wider and wider. I almost isolated myself within the process community. Because I was not a participant in my home community and family, I did not and felt I could not communicate with others who were not in training. I had made the training into a cult. I was looking to other people in the training group for their response so I could know if I was doing it (me) right. I used all my addictions during the training to distract myself in group when I began to hear things I needed to hear and did not want to hear. I used training to make myself feel one-down by constantly comparing myself to others in the group. I needed to do it right. I functioned on the edge of the group, observing and trying to learn what was happening so I could fit in, just like I did in my biological family. I thereby kept myself from participating and feeling fully.

I especially did my realtionship with Anne Schaef addictively. Notice I believed that relationships were something one did. I used her as my guru and alluded around her the aura of the teacher/leader not facilitator. I would not say what I experienced of her. I could not comment on our relationship. Using the one-down move, I experienced no relationship. It was easy in my position of one-down to criticize her or glorify her. I used my experiences of her to be part of an exclusive group with its own special language so I could feel accepted. I would only half listen to feedback from Anne and others, nodding my head in agreement with their experience before I checked with myself about what I knew.

It is good that the Living in Process training lasted a year. That year was long enough for me to be and to feel, experience, and begin expression of my feelings. I began to lose my tolerance for pain. I began to experience myself. I began to experience others. I began to know my boundaries, to know where my responsibilities stopped and others' responsibilities began. It seemed as if through osmosis I learned to begin recognizing, naming and being with myself.

That group process brought me to a place of participating in my work differently. When doing process groups through my private practice I became aware of the potential that existed to use the relationship addiction of group members for personal gain. Relationship and romance addicts are vulnerable people who often use group for identity as I had done. I began asking myself my motive. Did I own these people? I began asking if I was using them to fulfill my own pattern of being one-up or one-down. Was I facilitating their work? Was I enabling their dependence? I began asking if I was using clients to feed a money addiction. I also began asking if I was using clients for family. I am learning in my recovery to look at my motives. I ask myself what I do not want to feel when I get into compulsive doing. I am learning to ask myself what I need or want. I check in with myself often to know my feelings.

Addicts try to control and hold their world still. Nonrecovery is about being stuck. It is about nonliving. "Stop the world I want to get off" clearly states what addicts do. They stop or attempt to stop the living, changing world with illusions of control and other addictive characteristics as they express their addictive process.

I keep myself stuck in my work addiction by not

giving myself permission to stop a job once started or not to finish what I said I would do. I am learning to give myself that option. I noticed that my recovery from workaholism escalated after my process brought me through much deep work on incest issues. Recovery work is recovery from my history and shame. My family was a shame-based family. I was told "shame on you" when I did not do what was expected. Doing what was expected often meant leaving who I was.

The twelve steps of Alcoholics Anonymous have been borrowed by over two hundred and fifty recovery groups such as Alanon, Overeaters Anonymous, Debtors Anonymous and Sex and Relation Addicts. All of these groups rewrite the first step to include their particular addiction. The rest of these steps, two through twelve, remain intact and are applicable to other programs of recovery from substance or process addictions.

The steps for workaholics would thus be:

1. We admit we are powerless over our work addiction and doing and that our lives had become unmanageable.

2. Came to believe that a power greater than ourselves could restore us to sanity.

3. Made a decision to turn our will and our lives over to the care of God as we understood Him.

4. Made a searching and fearless moral inventory of ourselves.

5. Admitted to God, to ourselves and to another human being the exact nature of our wrongs.

6. Were entirely ready to have God remove all these defects of character.

7. Humbly ask Him to remove our short comings.

8. Made a list of all persons we had harmed and became willing to make amends to them.

9. Made direct amends to such people whenever possible except when to do so would injure them or others.

10. Continued to take personal inventory and when we were wrong, promptly admitted it.

11. Sought through prayer and meditation to improve our conscious contact with God as we understand Him, praying only for knowledge of His will for us and the power to carry that out.

12. Having had a spiritual awakening as a result of these steps, we try to carry this message to others, and to practice these principles in all our affairs.

When looking at the specific twelve steps, Step One holds a trap for the workaholic. To say I am powerless over my work addiction and it has made my life unmanageable is almost impossible for the nonrecovering workaholic. The workaholic believes and has proof that unmanagability is impossible because he or she applies effort, attention and time.

75

Powerlessness is not in a workaholic's vocabulary. Here I am talking about power over others in a business sense not the personal power one comes to know through working a program. I was afraid of my personal power.

In my home I only knew that power was used over someone. In my church there was that power too. I learned nothing from society about personal power. As a woman, I believed I was not entitled to it. I believed only men were entitled to personal power. My workaholism was used to sabotage my coming to my personal power. I could keep myself very unfocused with minute details of various projects and unable to focus all of my energies onto what was important to me. It is of value that I worked Step One around my relationship addiction, for I could see more clearly how that step applies to my workaholism and alcoholism. And so it goes with the other steps.

At the time of this writing I know of several Workaholics Anonymous twelve-step groups in the San Francisco, Boulder, Colorado and Indianapolis, Indiana areas. There may be others of which I am not aware. The reader may learn of Workaholics Anonymous meetings located in their area by calling the closest Alcoholics Anonymous office.

I heard a friend at one twelve-step meeting talk about her work addiction and how it helped her to picture her job inside a bottle. She went on to tell us there was no difference between the alcoholic using alcohol and the workaholic using work. It is the same. I have carried that image and it has been helpful to me.

I am also facilitated in my recovery by being

around people who are not using work addiction. Just as the alcoholic often changes friends as they recover, so too for the workaholic. Being around people who are gentle and respectful of themselves and their use of time provides good support for me.

The changes are subtle as I progress in my recovery. I am noticing my pace is slower. I smell food. I eat less. I notice colors. I sense temperature and environmental changes. I am experiencing more of my environment. I play, really play and enjoy. There is less of a division between play and work. Often they are the same. I experience people. I am emotionally present.

I am aware as I come to the end of this writing how important the process of this book has been in my recovery from workaholism and doing. This book was not a project. It was centering me.

Good Journey

AUTHOR'S REQUEST

I am interested in hearing from others who are naming and attempting recovery from workaholism for a sequel and a newsletter about men and women's recovery process. Contact can be made by mail through:

Counseling and Consultation Services
2200 John Wooden Drive
Suite 208
Martinsville, Indiana 46151

THE PROCESS OF COMING TO THIS WRITING
1. Allen Watts, *Taboo Against Knowing Who You Are* (Random House: New York, New York, 1979)

LEARNING THE PROCESS OF WORK ADDICTION
1. Anne Wilson Schaef, *When Society Becomes an Addict* (San Francisco: Harper & Row, 1987)

BEING THE CHILD OF WORKAHOLIC PARENTS
1. Melody Beattie, *CoDependent No More* (Center City, MN: Hazelden Foundation, 1987)
2. *Anne Wilson Schaef, Escape from Intimacy* (San Francisco: Harper & Row, 1989)

STOP THE WORLD I WANT TO GET OFF
1. Anne Wilson Schaef, *Co-dependence Misunderstood-Mistreated* (San Francisco: Harper & Row, 1986). pgs. 64-65

THE PROCESS OF THE DISEASE OF WORKAHOLISM AND RECOVERY
1. Charles Whitfield, *Healing the Child Within* (Pompano Beach: Health Communications, 1987)

MOVING FROM THE INSIDE OUT
1. Wilson Schaef Associates, P.O. Box 18686, Boulder, Co. 80308
2. *Alcoholics Anonymous*, 3rd ed. (New York: Alcoholics Anonymous, World Services, Inc., 1976)